Sports Illustrated
HORSEBACK RIDING

The Sports Illustrated Library

BOOKS ON TEAM SPORTS

Baseball	Football: Defense	Ice Hockey
Basketball	Football: Offense	Soccer
Curling: Techniques and Strategy	Football: Quarterback	Volleyball

BOOKS ON INDIVIDUAL SPORTS

Badminton	Horseback Riding	Table Tennis
Fly Fishing	Judo	Tennis
Golf	Skiing	Track: Running Events
Handball	Squash	

BOOKS ON WATER SPORTS

Powerboating   Small Boat Sailing
Skin Diving and Snorkeling Swimming and Diving

SPECIAL BOOKS

Dog Training   Training with Weights
Safe Driving

Sports Illustrated
HORSEBACK RIDING

BY THE EDITORS OF
SPORTS ILLUSTRATED

J. B. LIPPINCOTT COMPANY
Philadelphia and New York
1971

ISBN-0-397-00736-1 Cloth Edition
ISBN-0-397-00735-3 Paper Edition

Copyright © 1959, 1960 by Time Inc.
Printed in the United States of America
Library of Congress Catalog Card Number: 74-161580
Revised, 1971

Seventh Printing

Photographs from *Sports Illustrated*,
© Time, Inc.

Photographs on the cover and pages 10 and 80:
Richard Lerner

Photographs on pages 12–13, 16, 62, 63 and 95:
Jerry Cooke

Photographs on pages 24 and 79: *Tony Triolo*

Photograph on page 32: *Fred Ward, Black Star*

Contents

Text by Gordon Wright with Alice Higgins
Illustrations by Sam Savitt

1. POINTERS	11
RIDING IS FUN	11
LEARNING THE RIGHT WAY	14
PRIVATE LESSONS	14
UNDERSTANDING HORSES	15
2. HORSE AND TACK	17
THE HORSE	18
THE TACK	19
3. EQUIPMENT AND SEATS	25
WHAT YOU SHOULD WEAR	25
RIDING STYLES	27
POSITION IN THE SADDLE	27
4. HOW TO RIDE	33
ON THE GROUND	33
NOW—GET ON THAT HORSE!	36
GETTING A LEG UP	42
GETTING YOURSELF DOWN	44
PREPARING TO RIDE	49

Holding the Reins	50
Using a Crop	53
Adjusting the Equipment	54
Stopping and Backing	57
At the Walk	58
Guiding Your Horse	60
Posting the Trot	65
Sitting the Canter	72

5. THE CARE AND FEEDING OF HORSES — 81

How to Buy and Keep a Horse	81
Careful Selection	83
Behavior of the Horse	83
Physical Condition	84
The "Basic Wardrobe"	84
Boarding Your Horse	86
Insuring Your Horse	86
Home Care	87
A Clean Stall	87
Grooming Your Horse	89
Seasonal Problems	91
Saddling Your Horse	91
Securing the Bridle	91
After the Ride	93

Sports Illustrated
HORSEBACK RIDING

1
Pointers

RIDING IS FUN

MORE Americans of all ages are riding for pleasure today than at any time since the automobile replaced the horse. Whether you are six or sixty, you can learn to ride. The age at which you begin is not important, and the common belief that no one will ever be a good rider unless he starts as a child is erroneous. But what is important is the manner in which you go about learning. If you learn slowly and correctly you will ride well and your pleasure in the sport will be greatly enhanced. To achieve this, you should have a well-behaved horse and some supervision. Both are obtainable in most cities from livery stables and in the country at camps or from friends. You also will find that an advance understanding of what you and the horse do, separately and together, will make learning easier for both of you. That is the purpose of this book.

Riding is a year-round sport that offers endless variety. You do not need a partner or a group to enjoy it. A solitary ramble can be as pleasant as a jaunt with friends.

You *do* need to be able to manage your horse. Do not be misled by well-intentioned friends who may tell you there is nothing at all to riding and that you can teach yourself after a few tries. You are likely to spend several unhappy hours and form a number of bad habits before you are convinced to the contrary. For example, you may find yourself included in a group that knows how to ride and you may believe that your horse will follow docilely. Perhaps he will—but at an assortment of speeds that could make the trip pretty horrifying.

Learning the Right Way

If you go off alone and rent a horse without instruction, the stable may give you an animal that is familiar with the ways of inexperienced riders. In the ring old Nellie may simply march to the center and stand quietly dozing for an hour. If outdoors she may head off amiably for the park only to stop and eat grass at the first likely-looking spot, returning you safely when your money's worth of time is used up. Save your money and your temper, swallow your pride and learn correctly. Nellie will give you a great ride when you know how to ask her.

Most cities of any size have riding academies; consult your friends or your classified directory. Most academies will offer both private and class lessons, but not all of them, either in the city or country, will offer both. The quality of instruction will, of course, vary. If you have a choice, spend a day or so just watching. You can observe just how much attention the instructor gives the student, and in what manner it is given. Take the physical aspects of the establishment into consideration, too. An indoor ring means you can ride in all kinds of weather and at night.

Private Lessons

It is preferable to start with private lessons. They may seem costly—between five and ten dollars an hour is average —but it is money well invested in terms of pleasure, safety and competence for you. Private instruction is mandatory for small children and timid adults. It is best to begin by taking several half-hour lessons a week. Then, as your muscles become attuned, you can increase the time. After about ten hours of private instruction, the average person usually is able to start, stop and turn a horse, post a trot and have an idea about sitting the canter. The degree of skill acquired will, of course, depend on the individual, but *no one* is an expert rider at this stage.

Understanding Horses

There is no need to be afraid of horses, but one should be careful around them. If you have never known a horse "personally" before, approach him with an open mind. Do not be influenced by the behavior of humanized television horses and don't equate horses with dogs—a horse is not an overgrown, loyal Rover. He is a horse and as such has his own unique character and individual personality. And despite romantic legends, it is reassuring to remember that horses are not as smart as people. Care and not fear is the sensible attitude: most accidents are due to ignorance on the part of the rider. To cite just one hazard: in getting acquainted with your horse it is quite correct to offer him a lump of sugar, an apple or a carrot—but put it on the palm of your hand and hold your hand out flat. He will take it very nicely. If you hold it in the tips of your fingers you may lose a few.

Don't expect your first horse to resemble the glamorous animals of the movies and television. Remember that handsome is as handsome does. Reliable stables usually supply beginners with a horse which has been mellowed by age. There is an old saying that a green horse and a green rider make a very bad color combination. And as for the style of riding that horse, there are several. Gordon Wright, America's leading teacher of the equestrian art, feels that the basic principles illustrated in this book are fundamental to all of them.

2
Horse and Tack

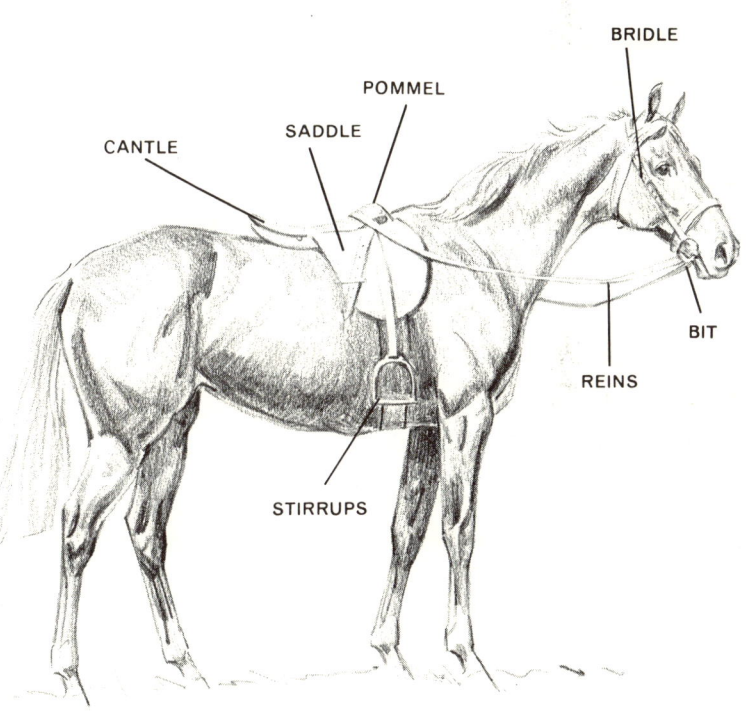

THE HORSE

IT is not necessary to know the name of every part of a horse's anatomy and of all the equipment he wears before you start riding. However, a little advance familiarity with these terms will make it easier to follow the directions of your instructor, and to follow the text of this book. The drawings identify most of the terms you will hear while you are learning to ride.

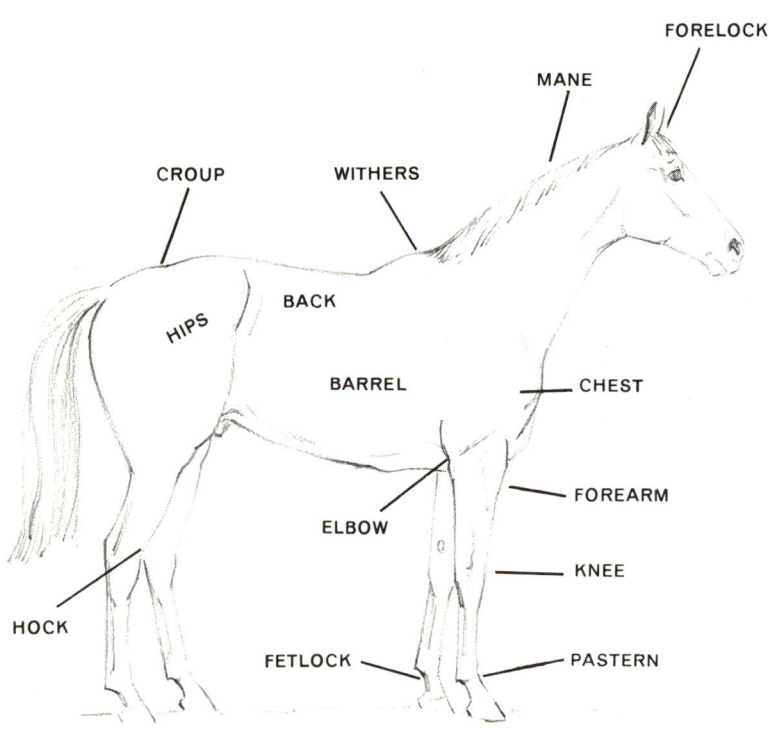

THE TACK

Let's start with the "suit" the horse wears—the "tack," as horsemen call it. It will be helpful to know how and why it is constructed as it is and to see why it works the way it does. You will note in the drawing that a standard English saddle is composed of several layers, each with a specific function. All saddles are made of wood covered with leather, and their main interior wooden support is called the tree. The girth is the strap (leather, linen or cord)

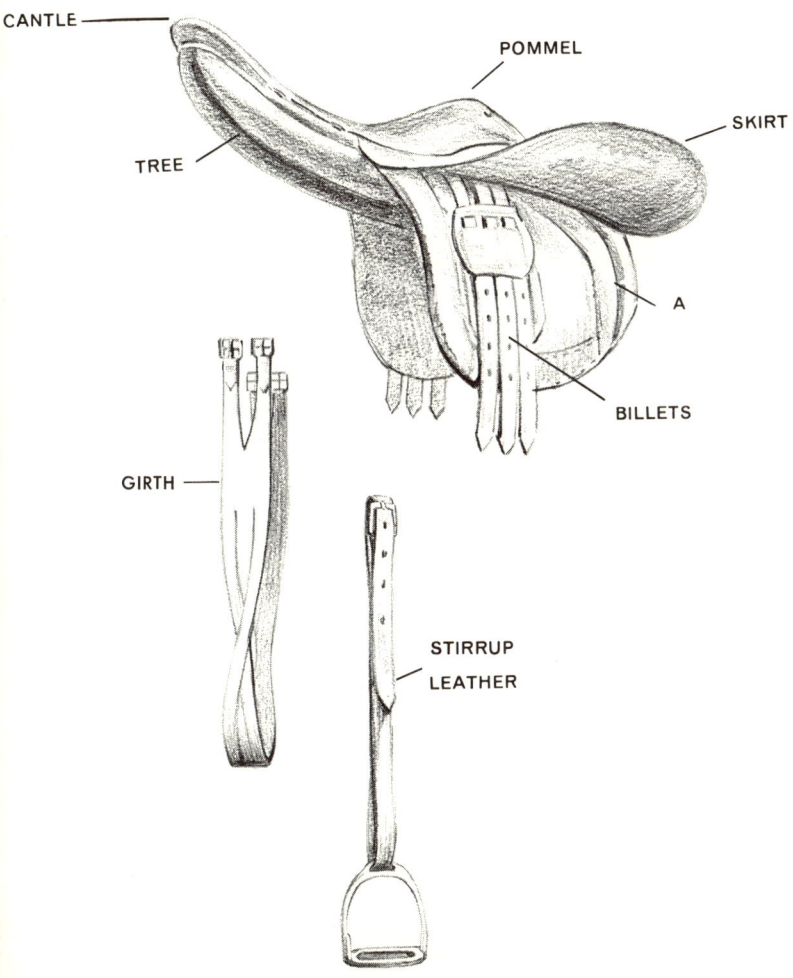

that is used to secure the saddle to the horse; it is buckled to straps on the saddle which are known as billets. Flap A protects the horse's side from being pinched by the buckles, and the skirt protects the rider's legs from the same thing, as well as from the horse's sweat. The stirrup is attached under the circular Flap C, and hangs down on the outside of the skirt. The stirrup leather has a buckle for lengthening or shortening. It should be slipped up under the flap after the length is adjusted. The leather is hung on a catch with either an open end or a hinged end (see the detailed drawing below). This is called a safety catch, and if pressure is applied to the rear of the catch the stirrup leather will drop off. Thus, if a rider's foot is caught in the stirrup when he falls, he cannot be dragged. Sometimes beginners push back for balance. When they do, this catch opens and the stirrup falls off. If this should happen to you, don't blame the saddle—blame yourself.

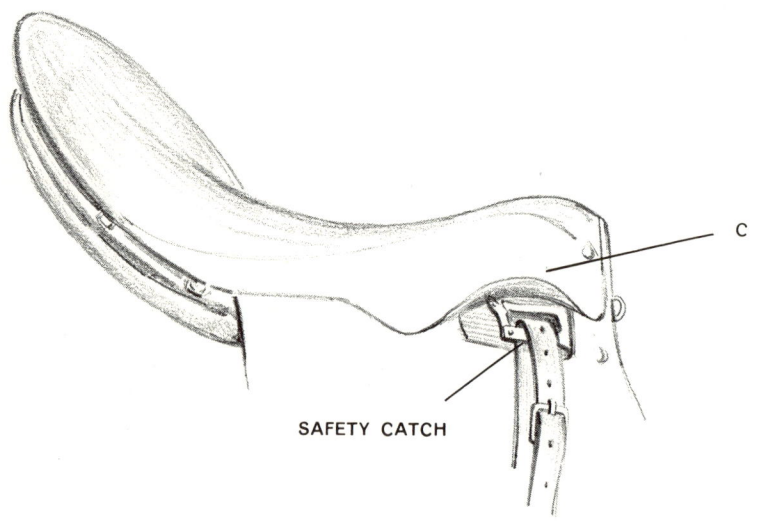

SAFETY CATCH

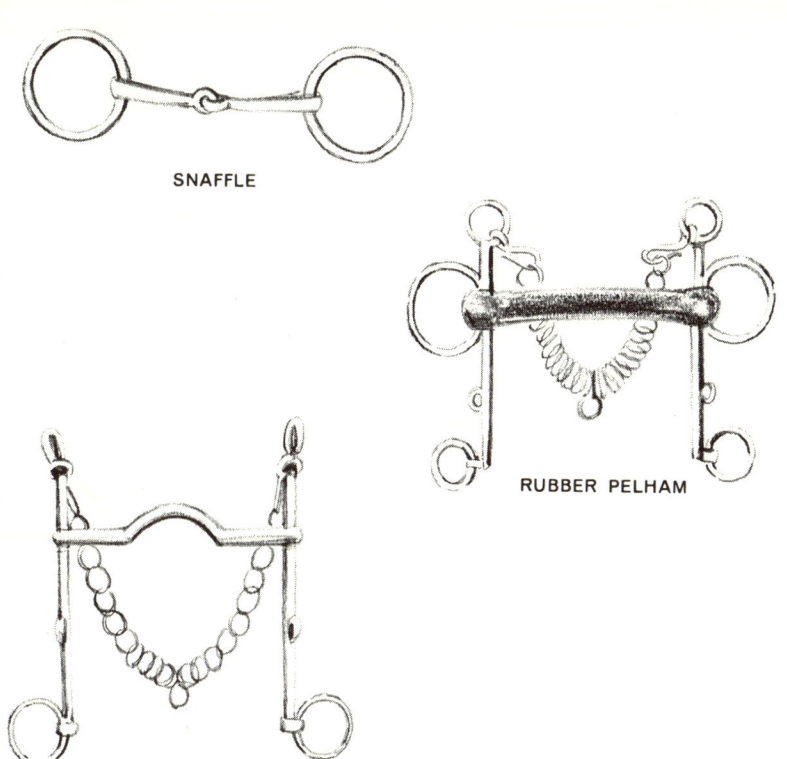

SNAFFLE

RUBBER PELHAM

CURB

The bridle is composed of a headpiece, a browband, a cavesson, cheekpieces, bits and reins. A horse's mouth has a gap between the front incisors and rear molars, and the bit (or bits) fits through the gap, resting across the tongue. There are many types of bits, but the basic ones used on an "English-type" horse are: (1) the snaffle, a straight bar hinged in the center and requiring only one set of reins; (2) the pelham, which is a single—but one with a short shank and a slight port, and a curb strap or chain. This bit requires two sets of reins; (3) the curb, a more severe bit, with a higher port, a longer shank and curb strap or chain, which is almost always used along with a snaffle. With this combination of two separate bits there are, of course, two sets of reins. Pulling on the reins applies pressure on the sides of the horse's lips and his tongue. With a curb, if the port is high enough, the pressure extends to the roof of his mouth, and via the curb strap or chain, against the back of his chin.

If you have studied all the drawings, you now should know the difference between a horse's withers and, say, his fetlock. Here are a few more general items that will make you feel knowledgeable when you arrive for that first ride:

A filly is a female horse under the age of four—and, in registered breeds, all birthdays are counted as January 1, regardless of the actual date. After a filly's fourth birthday, she is a mare.

A male horse is a colt until he is four; then he becomes a horse unless he has been castrated, in which case he is a gelding. Most male riding horses are geldings.

(The age of an unregistered filly, mare, colt, horse or gelding can be determined by his or her teeth, which is why the mouth is not the place to look a gift horse in.)

Horses come in an assortment of colors, some with special names. A black or brown horse is called just that. However, a brown horse (ranging in color from a light to a rich mahogany shade) with a black mane, tail and legs is called a bay. A horse of a brilliant red-gold, orange-copper or a dark liver color (or any color that would come under the term "red-headed") is called a Chestnut. Sorrel is a word for the same colors but is not often used, except in the West.

Most white horses are really faded greys. Grey horses are usually born black, with black skins; as they get older they get progressively whiter. A true white horse has pink skin.

Then there are the two-tone models—Roans, which

merely mean a sprinkling of white hair throughout the coat in Reds, strawberries, and greys. Spotted horses can be brown and white (pinto or skewbald), black and white (paints) or calico (bay and white—i.e., black, brown and white). The palomino—gold with a white mane and tail— is a breed as well as a color, as is the Appaloosa (any color, but with spots on his hindquarters). There are other variations of color and any of them can come equipped with white markings—stars, stips, blazes, and snips on the face, or stockings, socks, or coronets on the legs.

You will soon find that horses have as much individuality as people, in their color, conformation and personality, and before long you will smile condescendingly when some non-rider says: "All horses look alike to me!"

3
Equipment and Seats

WHAT YOU SHOULD WEAR

IT is not necessary to buy a $500 riding habit in which to learn, but clothes suited to the sport will help you, while the wrong ones can be a real handicap. When checking the stables in your area for instruction, note the style of jodhpur that is worn. It varies from place to place, depending on the type of horse, saddle and seat that is prevalent in the area. You can be correctly and comfortably attired in either the classic "peg-top" jod (page 26), or the Kentucky jod which has no bulge at the hip. The peg-top is generally worn by those who ride a hunter seat, whereas the Kentucky type is generally favored by the saddle-seat exponents. In either case, the right kind of clothing should be bought or borrowed before a foot is put into the stirrup.

Starting from the ground up, that foot should be in a boot or at least in a stout, laced oxford (jodhpur boots cost $10.00 up). Limber shoes, such as loafers or sneakers, develop bad habits and may even be hazardous. (Trying to keep the heel of this type of shoe from dropping off causes

tensions, and usually brings the heel up and the weight on the toe, which destroys balance.) Jodhpurs do not have to be tailor-made—a wash pair can be obtained for as little as $14.00—but they should fit well. If it is necessary to use blue jeans or Levi's, be sure to wear long underwear, no matter what the season. Unless you have this protection you are likely to wind up with raw knees which cannot be kept in proper riding position in an English saddle when posting the trot. A riding jacket is not essential to start with—any jacket of roughly hip-length that is roomy and not constricting will do. In these drawings we have eliminated gloves in order to illustrate the hands more clearly, but gloves should be worn—regardless of the temperature. A string or pigskin glove will help you avoid blisters.

Riding Styles

There are many styles of riding, some of them for highly specialized work, others merely faddish. As riding is largely a matter of balance and control, if you are properly instructed in the basics of handling both yourself and the horse at a walk, trot and canter in an English saddle, you will find no difficulty in later changing to a specialized type of riding if you so desire.

POSITION IN THE SADDLE

Gordon Wright points out that POSITION is the foundation of proper horsemanship. The correct arrangement of you in the saddle and on the horse can and should be learned at a standstill. Keep your head up and your eyes ahead; keep your back straight but not stiff, and the hands and arms flexible. Your seat and thighs are in close contact with the horse. The position of the foot in the stirrup and the length of the stirrup vary with the type of saddle and horse, but a study of the drawings of the main riding styles will show that these maxims are common to all of them. They include: 1. Gordon Wright's basic seat; 2. the Hunter seat—stirrups just a trifle shorter, body slightly more forward; 3. the Saddle seat—stirrups longer, and—since the stirrup is set back more toward the cantle—the seat a little farther back on the horse; 4. the stock-horse seat—the reins held in one hand, the left, as horses are taught to turn by pressures on the neck. (The right hand is free for throwing a rope to catch that calf.)

1. Gordon Wright's Basic Seat

2. The Hunter Seat

3. The Saddle Seat

4. The Stock-Horse Seat

4
How to Ride

ON THE GROUND

ATTENDANTS at livery stables and riding schools are likely to lead your horse up to a mounting block and summarily hoist you aboard. Don't let them. There is more to horsemanship than riding, and correct ground procedure should be learned first. A horse is traditionally approached and led from the left side, which is also known as the near side. Get acquainted with your horse by stepping up alongside the horse's left shoulder and taking the reins about six inches under the bit. Then, with your body facing the same direction as the horse, walk slowly forward. Look straight ahead—not at the horse. He will walk beside you or behind you and not on you. In this position you are safe from kicks and bites and still have control of the animal. The closer you stand to the horse the safer you are—the quietest will sometimes kick at a fly and hit you if you are in the way. There is no reason to fear your horse, but that does not mean you should take him for granted. Any horse is capable of inflicting injury, but most accidents are the result of the rider's carelessness or ignorance.

Arranging the reins

Control of the horse at all times is highly important, and this means keeping a firm hand on the reins. Now that you have walked your horse, you are ready to mount. The first thing to do is get the reins in order. They are of equal length, and there is a seam or buckle that marks the center spot. Find that seam and with the right hand pull the rein

2

so that the slack is taken up on the off side. Then bring the left hand up until it meets the right rein on the horse's neck just in front of the withers, and take both reins in the left hand. Be sure that the leftover reins, known as the bight, are neatly arranged alongside the shoulder of the horse so as not to get caught in the stirrup.

NOW—GET ON THAT HORSE!

In arranging the reins in your left hand, you have shifted the position of your body so that you are facing slightly to the rear. Your rein hand should be resting easily on the horse's neck, a few inches ahead of the pommel (placing your hand too close to the pommel can result in pinched fingers). Now, without letting go of the reins, open the fingers of your left hand far enough to get a handful of the horse's mane. This will give you more stability and will keep you from jerking the horse's mouth if at first you find yourself using the reins as a strap in pulling yourself aboard. Take the top of the stirrup in your right hand and turn it toward you, then thrust your left foot all the way into it—"home," as horsemen say—so that the metal is against the heel of your boot. You are now ready for two forceful movements—a hop followed by a spring. The hop off the right foot will swing you around to face the horse and enable you to grasp the cantle of the saddle with your right hand. The spring, also off the right leg, follows immediately. With a good spring an adult can stand up straight in the left stirrup, but if you are shorter, like the girl pictured here, you will have to pull with your arms as well. While performing this maneuver, keep the toe of the left foot—the one in the stirrup—pointed downward and the leg in close to the horse. Otherwise you may nudge the horse in his side with the toe of the boot. So now you are halfway there. Your weight is distributed between your arms and your left leg. Now lean on your left arm and move your right hand from the cantle to the off, or right hand, side of the pommel. At the same time swing your right leg over the horse's back and let yourself down into the saddle. Presto! You're aboard. Then place your right foot in the stirrup, take the reins in both hands and you are ready to ride. The process we have described here

(*continued on page 40*)

1

THIS SERIES OF DRAWINGS shows the actual steps involved in mounting a horse correctly. You will notice **(1)** that the rider holds some mane along with the reins. You can see **(2 and 3)** that the left hand drops a bit as the rider pulls to help herself up—but there is no change in the tension of the reins. If a sizable swatch of mane is held it does not hurt the horse, but jerking on his mouth will.

2

3

ONE OF THE CRITICAL MOMENTS in mounting a horse correctly comes **(4)** after you have straightened up in the left stirrup and are preparing to swing your right leg over the animal's back. The knee **(5)** should not be straightened until midway through the swing, and the toe pointed forward and up. This will save the horse from a kick in the rump, and the rider from possible loss of balance which in turn could result in a fall.

VIEW FROM ABOVE of mounting shows the position of the right hand after it has been moved from the cantle. The rider has not yet let herself down into the saddle. Note that the right ankle is cocked to help her leg clear the horse.

actually takes only about 10 seconds, but you will need to practice it a good many times to make all the motions smooth. Don't be discouraged if it seems awkward at first. Even a small girl, as these illustrations show, can learn to mount an average-sized horse easily—and without any assistance.

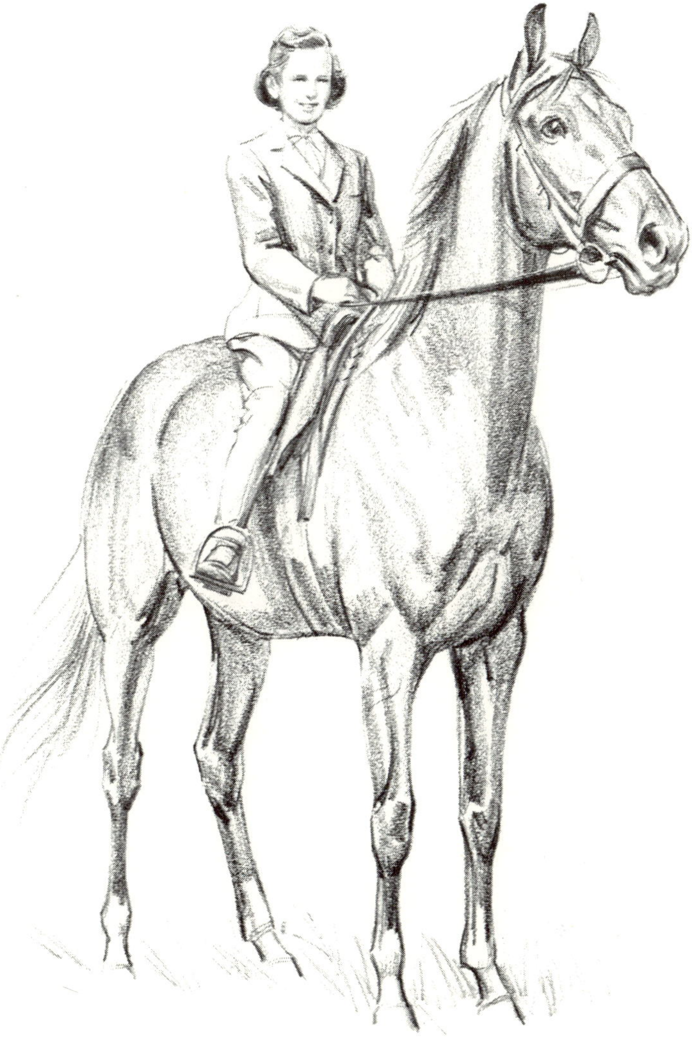

GETTING A LEG UP

Once you have learned to mount a horse unassisted, it is permissible to allow an instructor or friend to "give you a leg up." For this procedure, you again take the reins in the left hand and grasp the mane just in front of the withers. Place your right hand on the cantle, and stand close to and facing the side of the horse. Bend your left leg at the knee so your helper can grip it, as shown in the drawing at right. Then comes a combined and coinciding effort—you spring off your right foot and your aide boosts you upward, keeping your left leg and knee pressed close to the saddle. The lift must be high enough to allow your right leg to swing clear of the croup. Your right hand moves on saddle as when mounting unassisted.

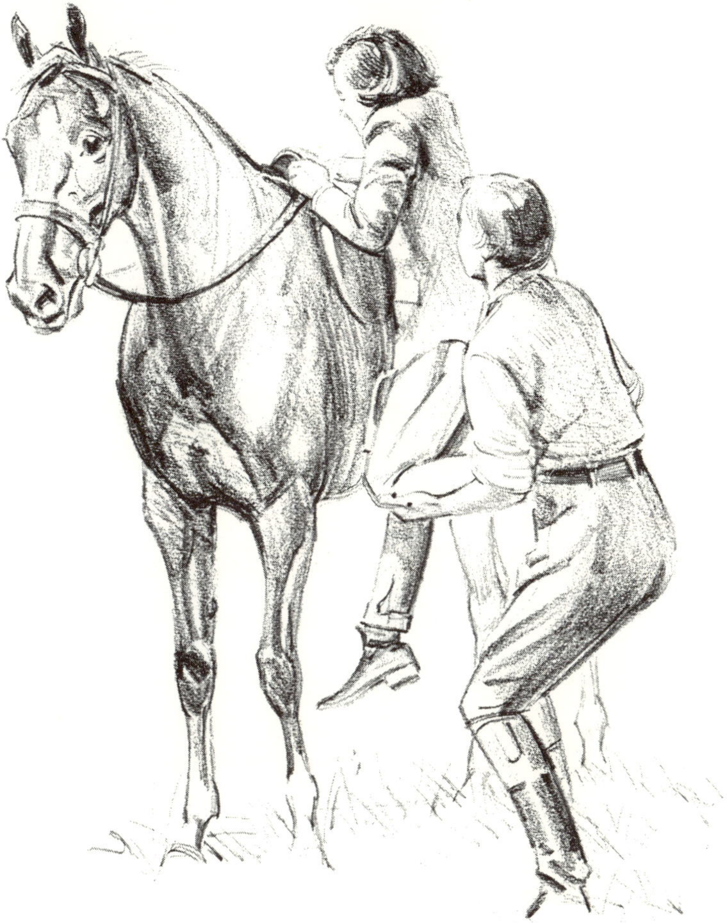

GETTING YOURSELF DOWN

Now that you're in the saddle, your next move—before the horse ever takes a step—is to get out of it. Dismounting is very much like mounting, only in reverse. Gather the reins in the left hand and place it on the horse's neck. Next, place your right hand below the pommel, remove the right foot from the stirrup and pass the right leg over the horse's back without touching it.

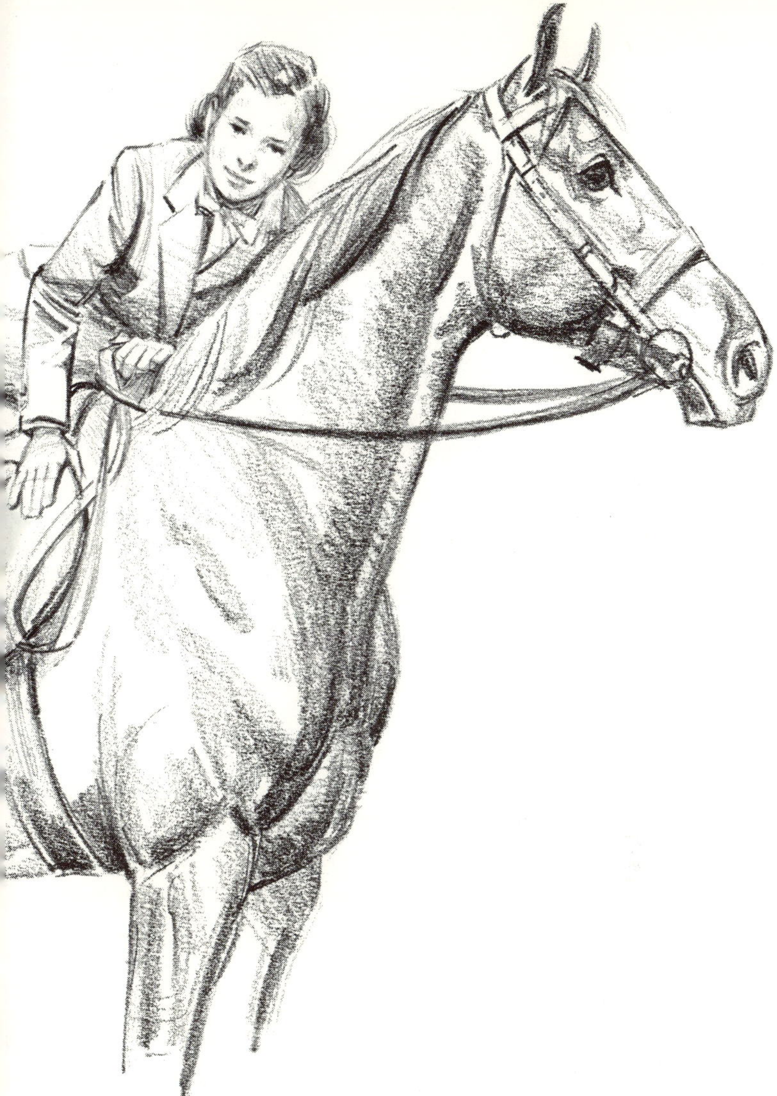

Shift your right hand to the cantle and keep the weight of your body on your hands. Remove your left foot from the stirrup and descend lightly to the ground.

Even when descending, you should be in a position to maintain control of the horse. Don't push yourself away from the animal, but slide down his side. Note the position of the right hand and arm. If the horse moves, you can shift your weight to that arm and have your left hand free to prevent movement.

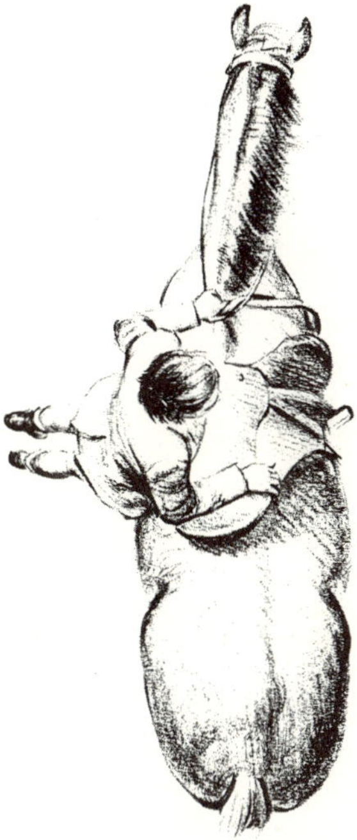

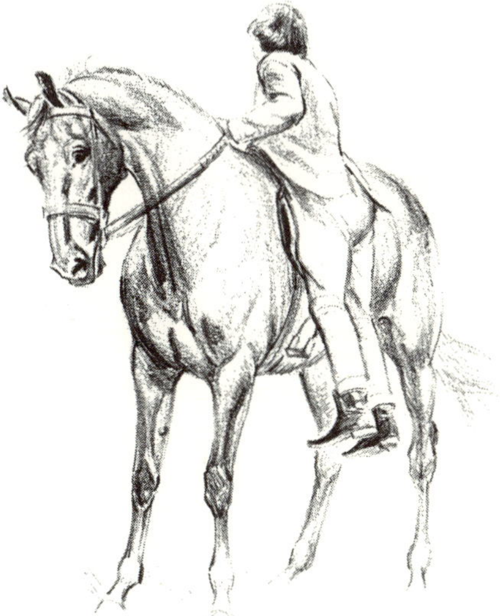

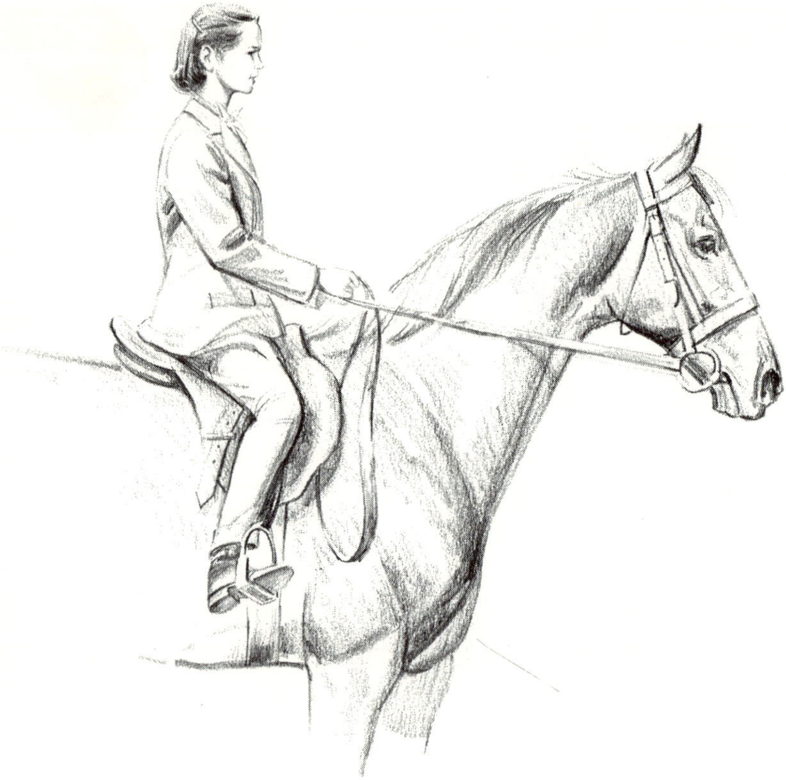

PREPARING TO RIDE

Having learned to mount and dismount, you are ready to start riding. But first you need to understand the proper arrangement and balance of the various parts of your body—in a word, position. You can achieve the proper position to be used in motion while the horse is standing still—it is basically the same for the walk, the trot, the canter. As we have stated, this is what you must do: keep your head up and eyes ahead; keep your back straight but not stiff and your hands and arms flexible; your elbows should be bent, with the reins held in front of the horse's withers, hands about two inches apart, and high enough to make a straight line from the horse's mouth to your elbows. Your seat and thighs should be in close contact with the horse. The ball of each foot is in the stirrup, with the heel down.

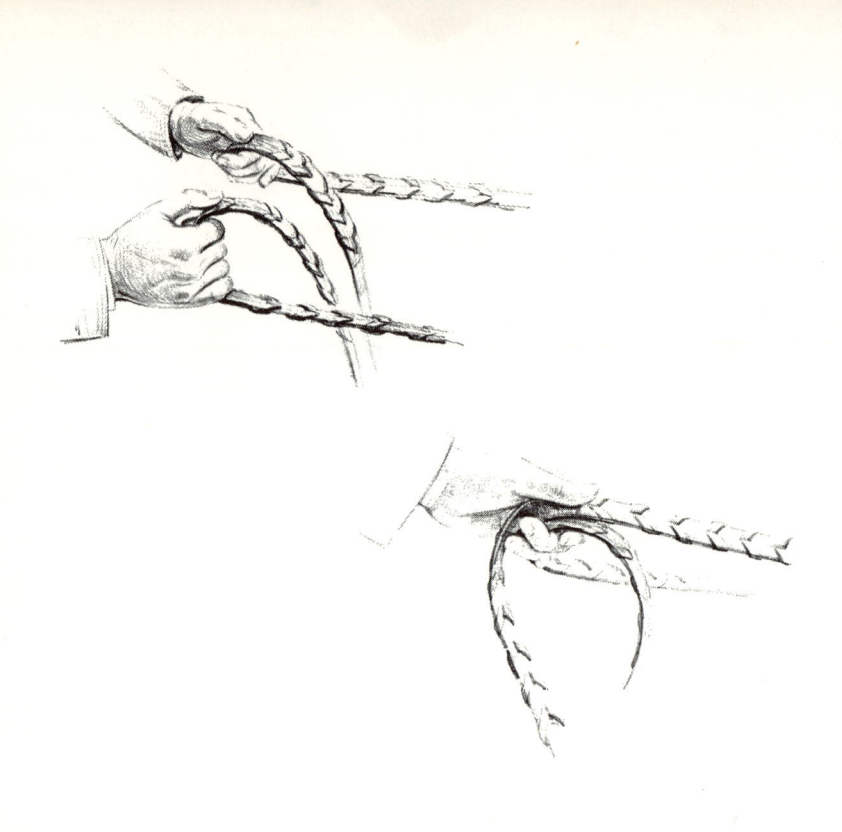

HOLDING THE REINS

Ordinarily you should keep both hands on the reins. However, occasions may arise when it is necessary to hold them in one—the left. The two drawings above show how to hold the single rein, or snaffle, in both hands or in one. The drawings at the right show how to handle double reins. The top rein is still the snaffle, and the second is called the curb. Draw the snaffle through the palm of the hand. Hold it firmly between the thumb and the middle joint of the forefinger. To transfer the rein from the right hand to the left, pass the right hand behind and under the left and slip it into the palm of your hand.

To hold the double reins, loop the snaffle around the little finger. Loop the curb rein around the second and third, holding both between the first and second. To shift double reins, place the right hand behind the left and slip the left forefinger between the snaffle and the curb reins.

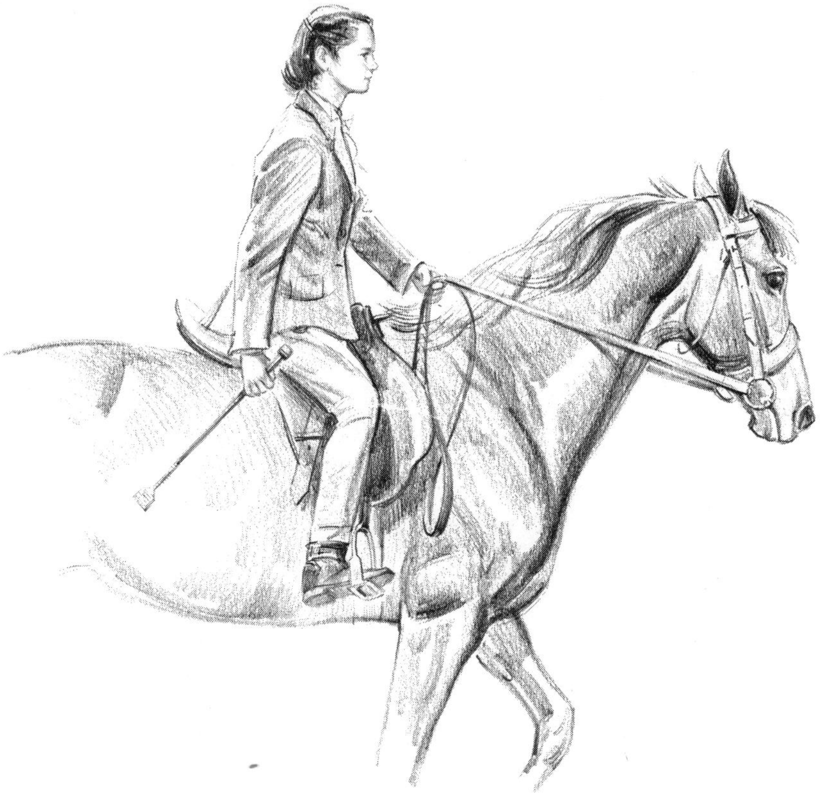

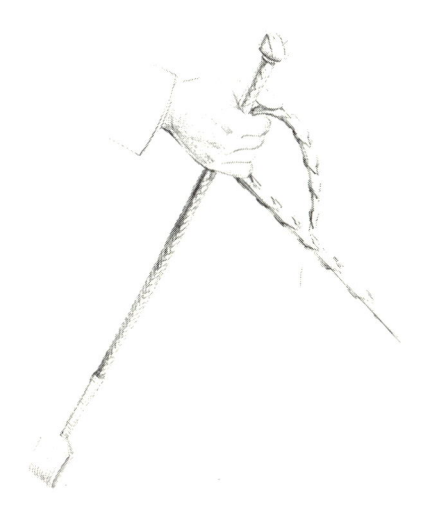

USING A CROP

You will not need to use a crop until you are ready to trot or canter, so for the sake of clarity we have not in general shown one in the rider's hand. The crop (also called bat, whip or stick) is an aid, as are your voice and legs, to urge the horse onward. Not all horses need to feel a crop; for some, simply seeing one in the rider's hand is enough inspiration. You will note that the crop is carried in the right hand, along with the rein (see above). If you need to use it, take the rein in your left hand (see opposite), making sure that you have and can maintain control. Then use your bat briskly behind the girth.

ADJUSTING THE EQUIPMENT

If you feel your saddle slipping, stop. Put your left leg in front of the saddle on the horse's shoulder, with your weight in the right stirrup and the reins in the right hand. Fold the skirt of the saddle forward under your calf, as shown below, or over your thigh. The straps on the saddle to which the girth is buckled are called billets. Take hold of a billet and pull upward, past the desired hole, then let it slip back into position. Do the same thing with the other billet, making sure that both billets are flat when you have finished.

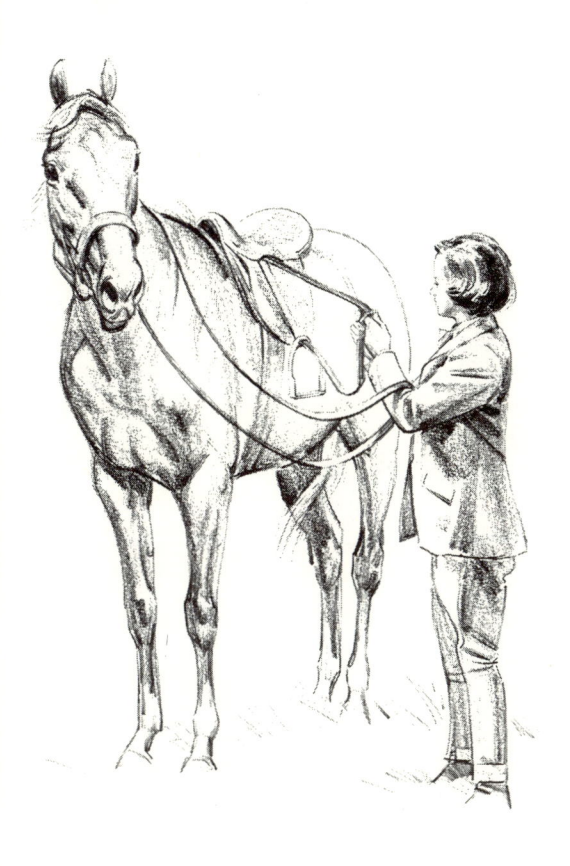

TO SHORTEN or lengthen the stirrup before mounting, loop the reins around your left arm; then reach up under the flap and pull the buckle downward—it works like any belt buckle. After adjusting to the proper length, check to see that the buckle is fastened; then pull downward on the understrap and the buckle will slide into place.

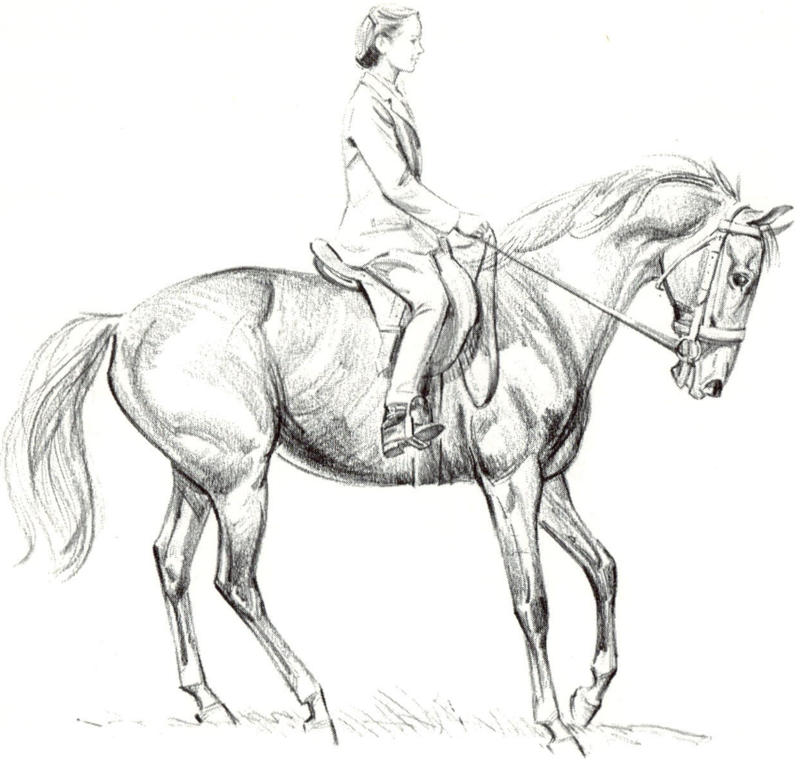

STOPPING AND BACKING

Stopping a walking horse is easy, if you know how. (Actually, the type of horse you will be riding at this stage requires little encouragement to stop.) When you are ready, close your hands on the reins; the little fingers exert a squeezing action which increases the pressure on the reins and on the horse's mouth. This alone may bring him to a halt, but if it does not you should increase the pressure. Now that your horse is halted, try backing him. Use your hands in the same manner as you did when pulling to a halt from a walk. You will feel the horse's weight shift from the fore to the hindquarters before he starts moving into reverse. Give him time to make that shift. He will back a few steps. Ease off the pressure when he has stopped. That is his reward.

AT THE WALK

Now you are ready to move, but before you do you must know several things about controlling your horse once he is in motion. You start and then maintain control by the proper use of the natural aids, which are your hands, your legs—and your seat. To start, hold the reins lightly but firmly so you have a direct, "feelable" contact with the horse's mouth. Nudge the horse gently with your legs. Your horse will begin to walk. Use your legs to prevent the horse from stopping, and your hands to restrain him from moving into a faster gait.

GUIDING YOUR HORSE

The next thing is to learn how to steer your horse so that you can ride where you, and not the horse, care to go. At first you will feel a terrible temptation to look down at yourself and the horse—just as a novice dancer wishes to watch his feet. Don't do it. Look ahead at where you are going; this not only helps keep you in the correct position, but when you turn your head in the direction you wish the horse to go the subtle change in your weight helps direct him. By doing these things correctly you will set the scene for the use of the most important aid—the reins. You have already established a light contact with the horse's mouth—evenly in each hand. Now to turn left pull the left hand slightly toward your body, thus putting more pressure on the left side of the horse's mouth. (To oversimplify slightly: if the horse's head is facing the way you want to go, the rest of the horse will follow. A well-schooled horse does not need to have his head pulled around, but occasionally the beginner will encounter an animal with an active interest in returning to the stable to munch hay. You can stop him. Keep aiming him where *you* want to go.) Try your turns first in the simplest manner, at a walk both to the right and left. Next, try circles to the right and left. Be sure you look in the direction that will close the circle.

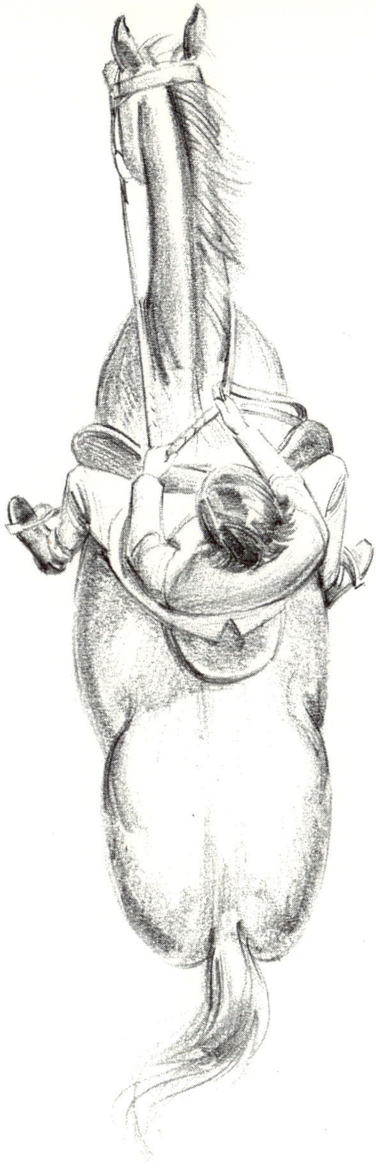

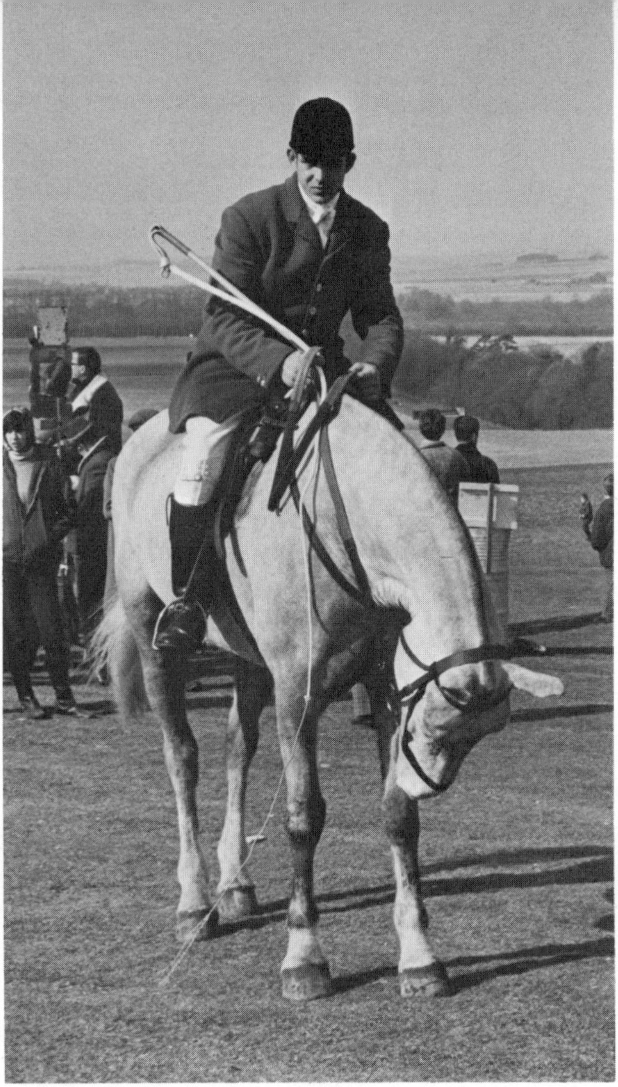

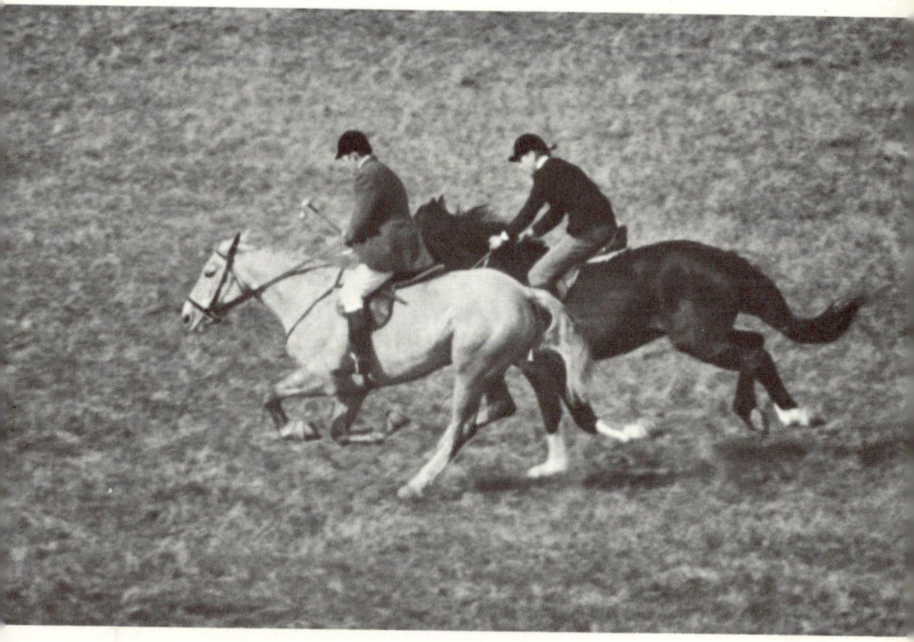

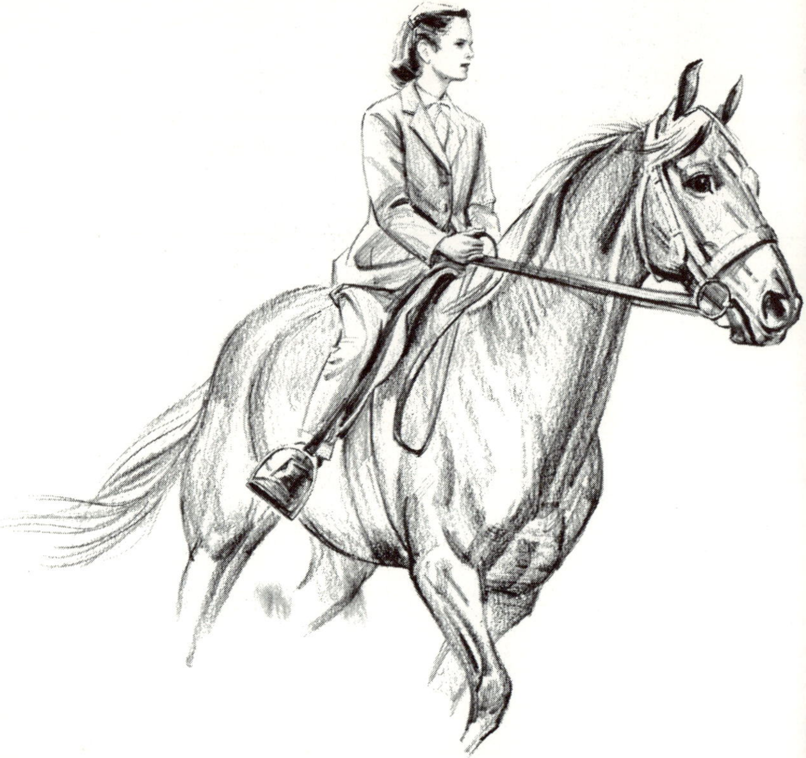

POSTING THE TROT

Once you have mastered yourself and your horse at the walk and are able to turn, stop and back, you are ready to progress to the next gait: the trot. This means that you must learn to post—the up-down, up-down movement that is so often misunderstood. It is no affectation but an aid and comfort to both horse and rider. When a horse trots, his legs move in diagonal pairs, making a two-beat rhythm as the hoofs hit the ground. The forward propulsion, or push—both for the horse and you—comes from *behind*, which is important to understand as it affects your movements and position in the saddle at all gaits. To start the gait use your leg or heels—your horse will go from a walk into a slow trot. For a few moments just sit there letting your knees and ankles act as shock absorbers. You will feel a bump, bump against your backside as the pairs of hoofs hit the ground, pushing or jolting you out of the saddle. Now, using those same leg aids, urge your horse into a faster trot. The jolt is far more pronounced, and you will thump that saddle at a more rapid rate as those diagonal pairs of hoofs hit the ground faster and faster. Time to start posting. This is what it means: when a pair of legs moves forward you are pushed forward and upward by the movement. You help by using your muscles, particularly in the thigh, and hold yourself in the air while the hoofs strike the ground, thus avoiding the jolt, then let yourself down so you can be pushed forward and up again (see illustrations on pages 66–67). You will note from the drawings that you do not stand up in the stirrups or heave yourself out of the saddle. Actually, the horse does most of the work by giving the push while you practice to develop the timing and coordination. Obviously, it is possible to post with either set of legs, which is what is meant by being on the right or left diagonal. To change diagonals simply sit through one bounce and catch the next push up. You're then on the opposite diagonal.

IN THIS SEQUENCE, the blackened foreleg indicates how you can tell which diagonal you are posting with by watching the horse's shoulder. If you are down when the right shoulder is back then you are on the right diagonal. Note also the bounce of the horse, indicated by broken line, as all four feet leave the ground at the trot's fullest extension. (Don't be confused: right or left does not mean right or wrong.)

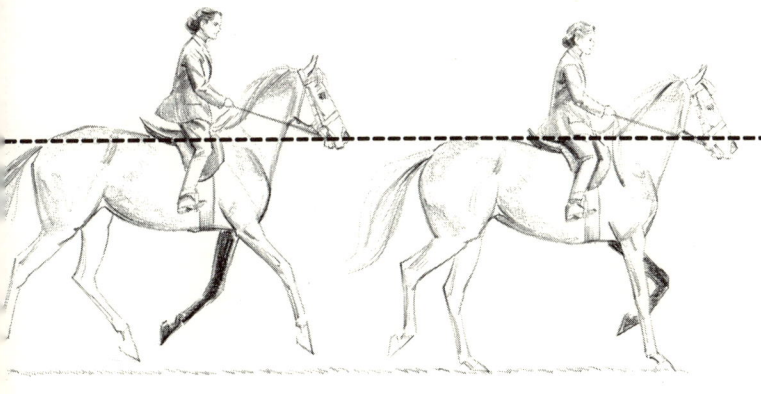

Starting to post, you move forward and up from your original position (*dotted line*) as the horse goes into a trot. The forward motion of the horse's hind legs gives you the push that helps make posting less of an effort and more comfortable for rider.

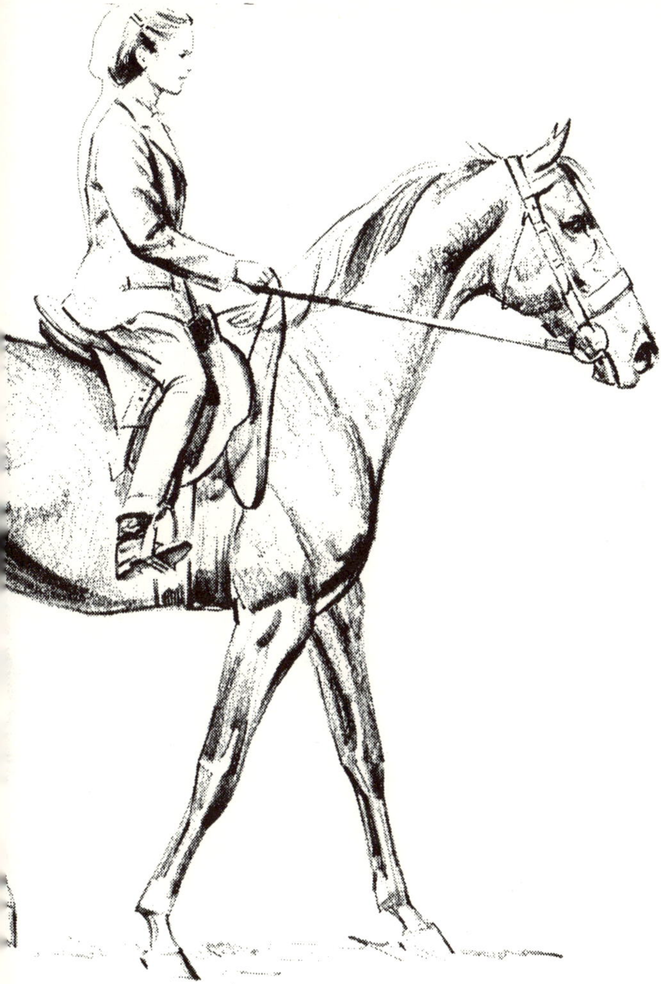

At the peak of the post, your seat is well off the saddle as the diagonal pairs of hoofs strike the ground, thus sparing you the jolt of the impact. Your knee is the hinge and, along with the ankle, provides you with a natural shock absorber.

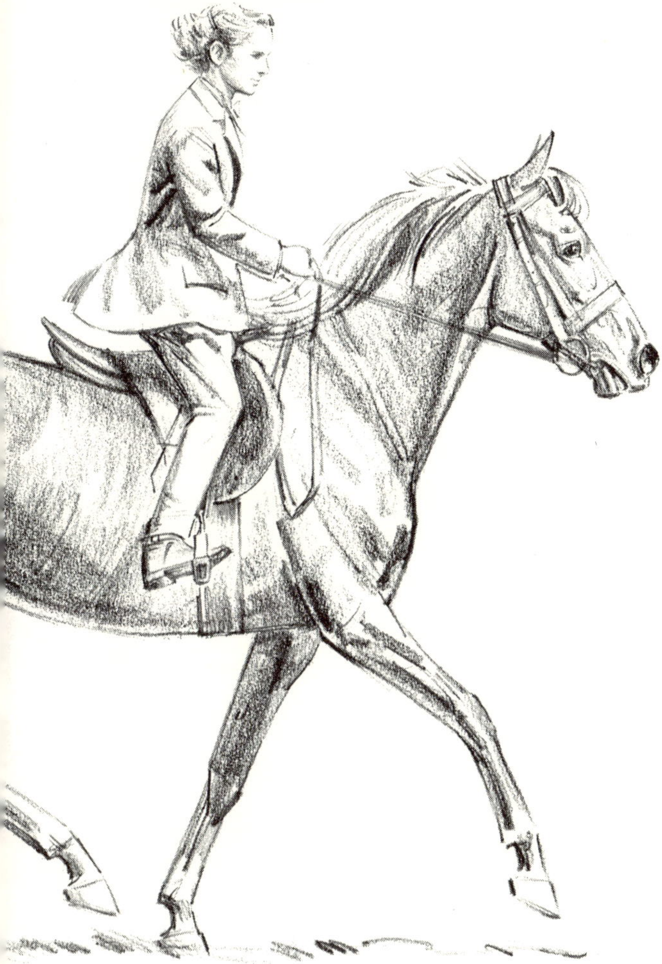

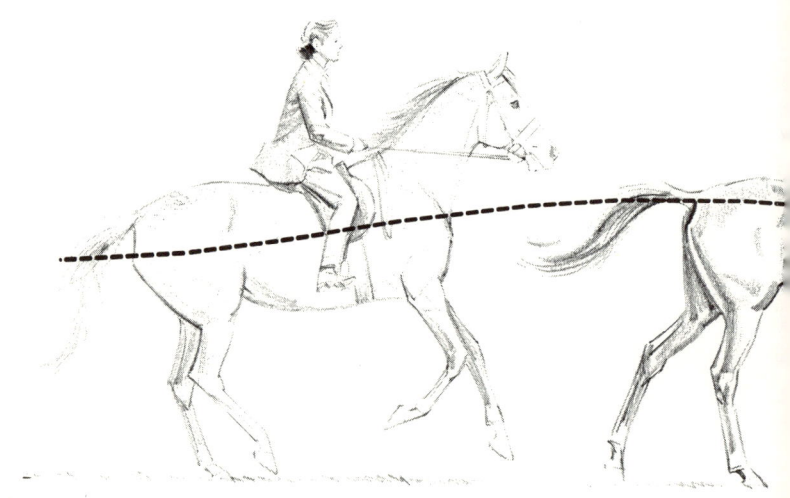

SITTING THE CANTER

You have learned how to get yourself *out* of the saddle when posting the trot; now it is time to learn how to stay *in* the saddle at the canter. The canter, lope or hand gallop is the third of the natural gaits of the average horse and is traditionally described as a three-beat gait. These drawings

72

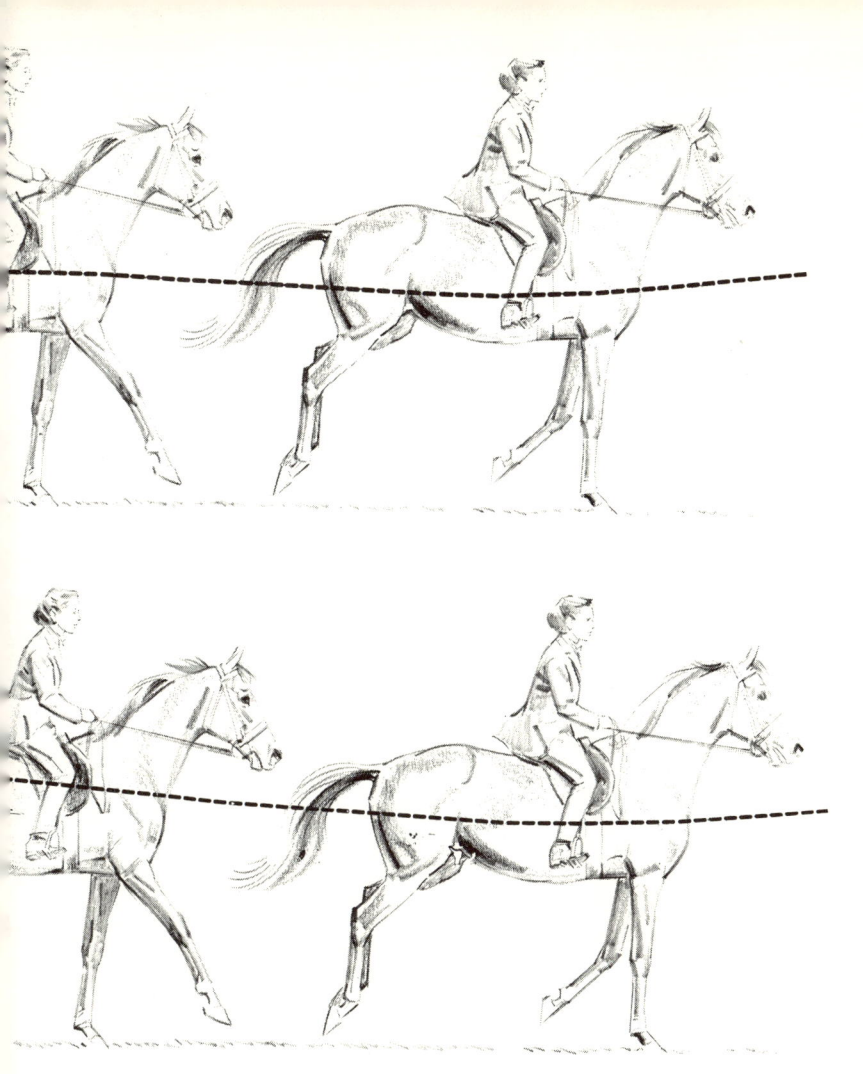

show a simplified version of what happens when a horse is cantering. Notice that he starts out on the left hind foot, rolls onto his left front and right rear foot, then onto his right front foot. (Of course, this pattern of footfalls can be executed in reverse, starting with the right hind foot, etc. This is known as cantering on different leads, as one of the front legs seems to be leading the movement.)

You can make your horse canter either by urging him on from a slow trot or, with some horses that have been trained to canter from a walk, by turning his head slightly and shifting your weight over the opposite shoulder. Once he is cantering, *relax*. Stiffening your backbone or pushing your weight down into the stirrups will send you bouncing

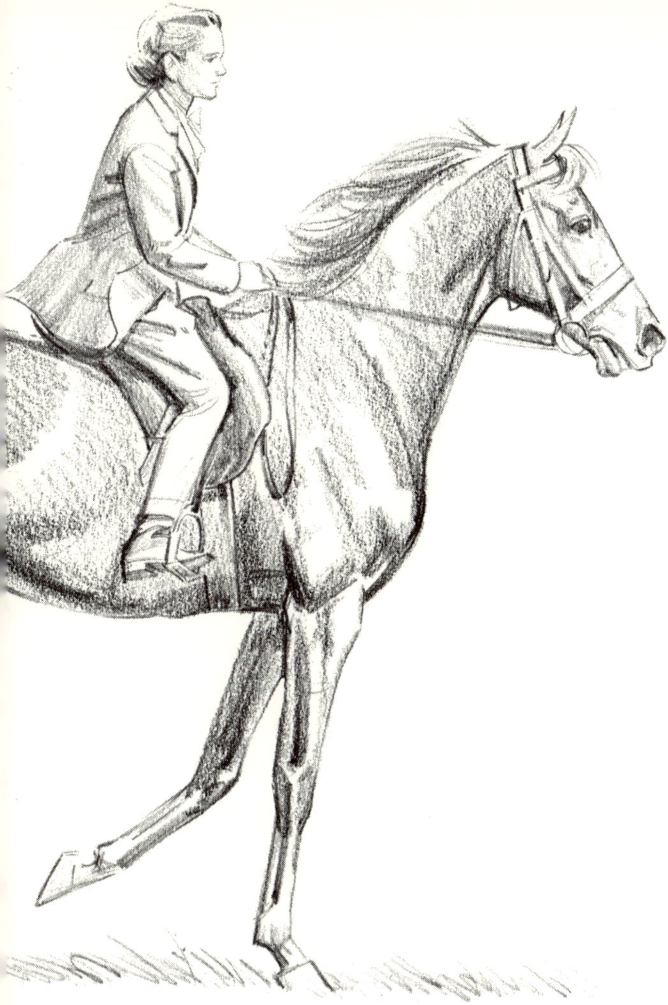

out of the saddle. You probably will pound the saddle for the first few strides while you adjust to the new rhythm and the impression of speed. But once you are with the horse you will find this rolling movement of the canter the greatest pleasure to ride. If at this time (or any other time in riding) you should lose your stirrup *don't* look down to try to find it.

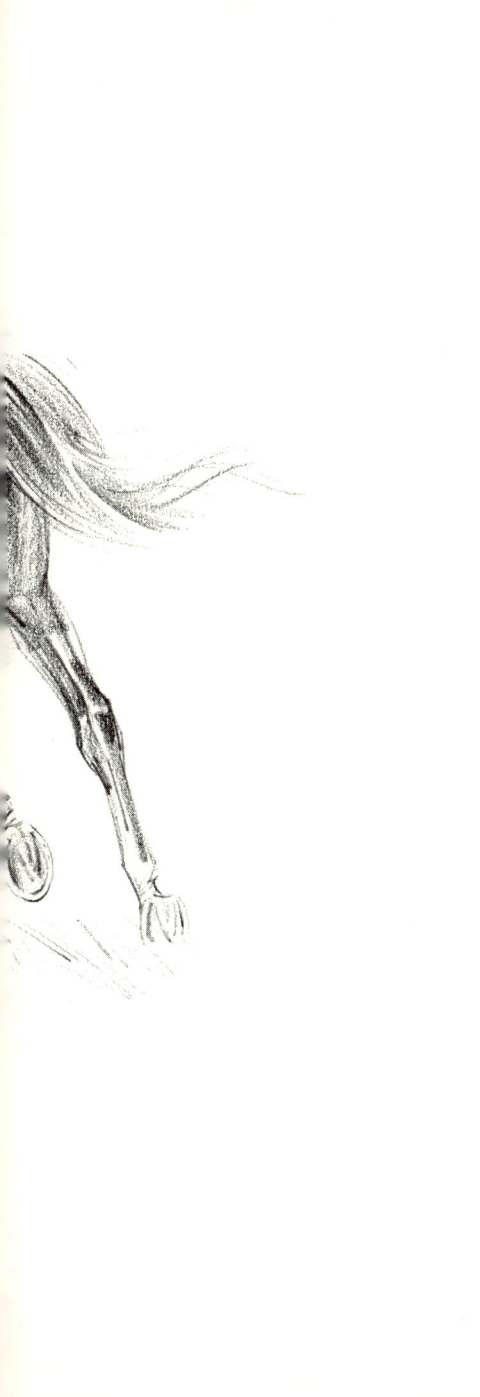

Keep those eyes looking ahead at where you are going, and that, in turn, will help you keep your balance. Keep your foot in position and you probably will catch the stirrup with no difficulty. If you have mastered these two lessons, you should be capable of riding a well-broken horse with safety and comfort.

At the canter you will find that the upper part of the body is slightly more forward than at the walk. If you move from a trot into a canter remember to come down to a slow, sitting trot and also use your legs to urge the horse to change gaits.

Remember, close contact with the saddle is necessary at the canter. Also notice that the turning principles at a faster gait are the same as at the walk. Using the reins, the rider looks in the direction of the turn, applying a light leg pressure to aid the horse.

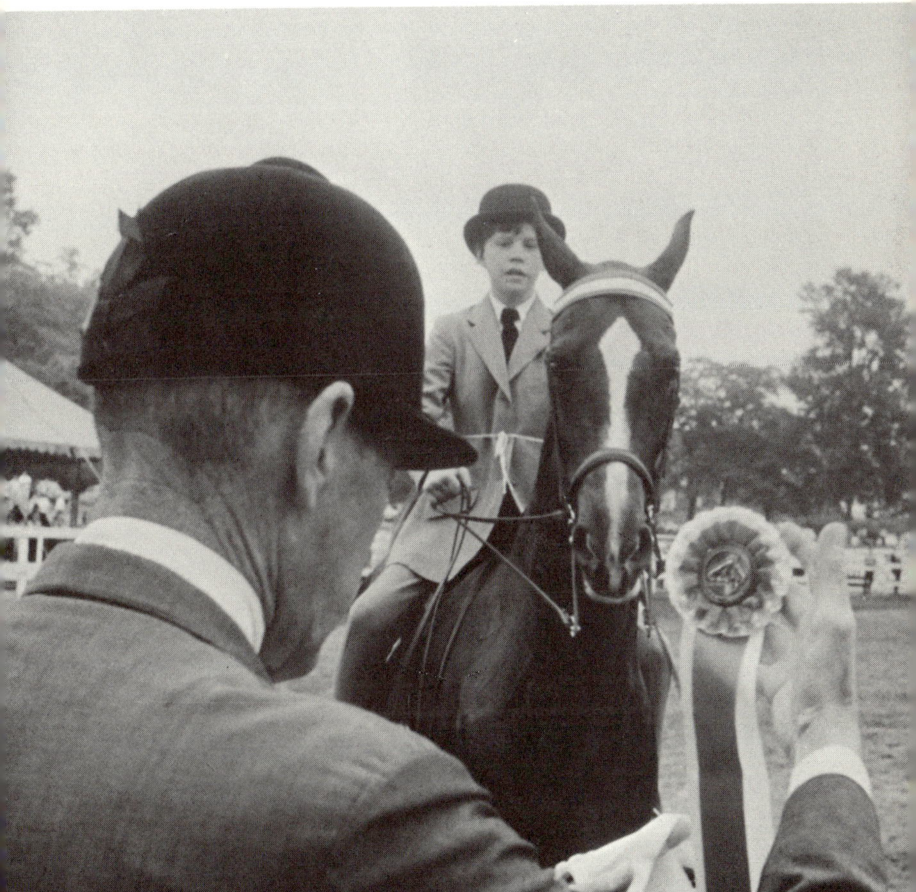

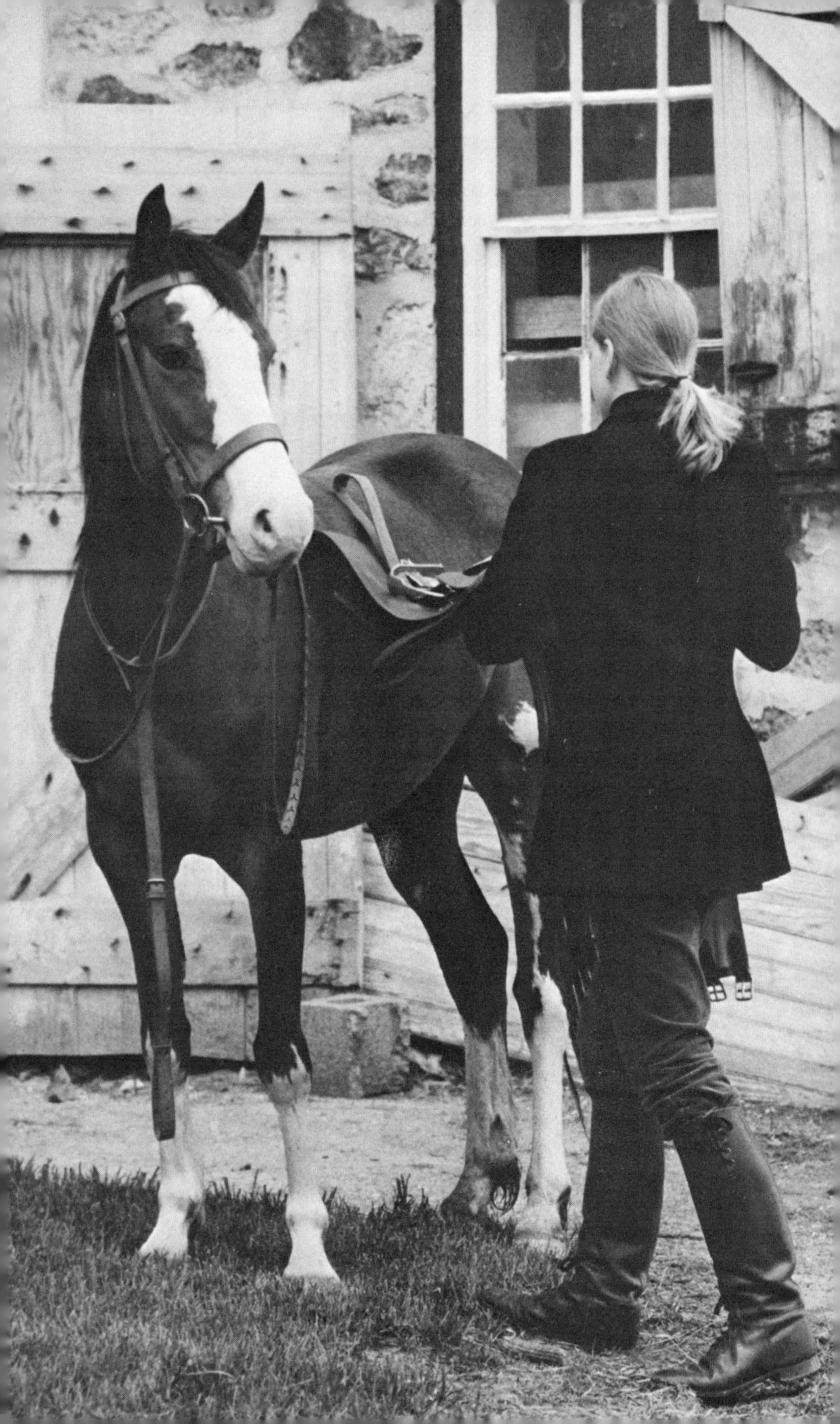

5
The Care and Feeding of Horses

HOW TO BUY AND KEEP A HORSE

NOW you have mastered the basic elements of riding and may be thinking of buying a horse of your own. If you are planning to buy a pleasure horse he should be just that—a pleasure to ride and to own. He (she or it) can be any one of a number of breeds, or of no particular breed at all. (Horsemen call the mongrel a cold-blooded animal, but he often has a warm and constant heart.) If he has the characteristics you are looking for—manners and soundness *above all* for real pleasure—his ancestry does not matter. Fortunately for the horse-shopper, the U.S.A. probably boasts the largest assortment of breeds, styles of riding and types of saddles in the world. By now you should have a good idea of the type that suits you and your locality.

If you are going to be a city rider on park bridle paths and tanbark rings, you probably will prefer a horse with the three normal gaits—the walk, trot and canter, and you will want English tack. Any well-mannered, nice-looking animal will suit your purpose. However, if you would be happier with a "name-brand," shop around among the American Saddlebred horses, Thoroughbreds, Morgans and Arabians. Perhaps you are planning weekend trail rides and pack trips and living in a community that rides "western." The quarter horse is the aristocrat of western breeds, but the Palomino or Appaloosa may suit you just as well.

Careful Selection

If you have been taking riding lessons at a public stable, you will have had a chance to see what is available—and at what price. You also can visit sale barns and farms, some of which have all types of horses for sale, where you will be allowed to watch the horses work and, if one strikes your fancy, try it out. Buying a horse at an auction is exciting, but can often be unsatisfactory unless you are acquainted with the animal on which you are bidding. Examine a bargain carefully—there is generally just as good a reason for a low price on a horse as there is for a cut-rate used car.

A riding horse reaches maturity by the time he is seven years old. However, do not be skeptical about buying a mount with "a little age on him," as long as he is reasonably sound and is *well-mannered*. An experienced horse can teach an inexperienced rider a lot. A ten- or twelve-year-old horse, if he has been properly treated, should have a good deal of mileage left. Many horses have been hunted, a vigorous activity, until late in their teens or even early twenties. Care and condition, past, present and future, will determine the span of usefulness—barring drastic accidents, of course.

Behavior of the Horse

When you spot an animal that appeals to you, ask to try him out. He should stay at a walk until asked to change gait—a horse that is constantly pulling may look showy, but is no pleasure to ride for very long. Sluggishness should also be avoided. It is discouraging work to make a listless horse respond. The goal is an alert but obedient animal. (Remember to take into consideration the time of year in which you are trying out the horse, if he is a stranger to you. The most wide-awake horse in the barn may be most indifferent on a hot, humid day, and the first cold snap may put new life into some old dog—temporarily.)

If you plan riding with a group discover how your prospective mount behaves around other horses. He may be all docility by himself, but obsessed with an urge to kick any horse that comes into his vicinity.

Find out if the horse will back, if he leads well, if he will stand tied, and if he will get into a truck or trailer (you *might* want to ship him some day). Ask about his disposition around the barn. Can you enter his stall safely? Does he have any vices such as cribbing (a nervous habit of chewing on the wood of his stall, not unlike fingernail biting in people).

Physical Condition

There probably is no such thing as the perfect horse, but your horse should be serviceably sound if you are going to enjoy him. Even experienced horsemen occasionally make mistakes about soundness, so if you are genuinely interested in buying a certain animal, call in a veterinarian to look him over. If the owner or his agent has guaranteed the horse as sound and the vet finds this to be true, you pay the bill (from $20.00 to $35.00). It is worth it. If the vet finds that the horse is not sound, the owner pays the bill. One word of warning: have the terms completely understood before the veterinarian is called, and call him only if you are *seriously* interested in the purchase. Then, even if it costs a little more, try to lease the horse with an option to buy, and learn to live with him a month or so.

The "Basic Wardrobe"

Once you have chosen your horse, you must then buy the necessary tack and equipment. Whether you plan on keeping him at a public stable or at home, you must have a "basic wardrobe" for him. Be sure that the saddle ($175.00 up) fits both you and the horse. Saddles, even of a certain type, will vary. This is also true of the bridle ($30.00–$45.00); inquire as to what kind of bit or bits your horse is accustomed to. It is worth getting a good halter, since this is the piece of equipment your horse wears most (a halter and leather lead will come to about $20.00–$25.00). Take a rough measurement of your horse before you go shopping, as blankets come in different lengths (a good 72-inch blanket sells for $35.00 and a 78-inch one for $37.00). You will probably also want a cooler (about $23.00) and a sheet for the summer ($13.00–$20.00). Sooner or later you will need a tack trunk to store the blankets in the summer, odd brushes and straps; they come in all sizes and prices, depending on your needs. Of course, many items in this "basic wardrobe" are available second hand—a good way to save money.

If you are not certain you can afford a horse, remember that the initial price of horse and tack is only the beginning. Unlike the family automobile, a horse consumes fuel even when he is not being used. Board bills will vary, depending on the locality, but probably will range from $100.00 to $200.00 a month. Training and exercising will cost more; if you are a weekend rider, you should make some arrangement to have your horse exercised regularly throughout the week.

Boarding Your Horse

Inquire about the services included in the price of the monthly board. Most stables will feed, groom, and clip your horse, clean your tack, and provide any minor medical treatment required (slight cuts, colds, etc.). If your horse develops a serious ailment the stable manager will call in a veterinarian—but at your expense. You also will get the bill for any tooth trouble your mount develops; in older horses sharp teeth are not uncommon and need to be "floated" (filed). A well-run stable also will see that your horse is shod when necessary—again the bill is yours. The number of new shoes will depend upon the amount of use the horse gets and over what type of terrain. A cinder bridal path will wear shoes faster than dirt or tanbark, but in any case you can safely figure several sets a year. (The price will vary; it will depend on the local blacksmith, and on whether your horse takes a keg shoe or has to have a custom-made job to correct a defect or enhance his way-of-going. A rough estimate is $25.00 a set and up.) Most horses need their shoes reset about every six weeks. Hoofs, like fingernails, grow. The shoe is taken off, the hoof pared down, and the same shoe put back on. (Resetting usually costs about $10.00.)

Insuring Your Horse

You may decide to insure your horse; the stable will have the name of a reliable broker if you are not acquainted with one. There is, however, no way to insure a horse against accidents, lameness or illness—only death. Unless you have some high-priced breeding stock, or unless you plan to ship your horse frequently, insurance probably is unnecessary. *But*, if you plan to let friends and neighbors ride your horse, look into liability coverage for yourself. Your best friend could fall off, suffer shock, humiliation and a scratch on the arm and sue. If best friend sues, you will probably lose, judging from cases which have come before juries.

Home Care

Want to keep your horse at home and care for him yourself? Well, remember one thing: complete care will take almost all of your spare time. Other than the basic wardrobe you already have acquired for your horse, he will need buckets, curry combs, brushes, a sweatscraper, water heater, clippers, saddle soap, sponges, a hoofpick, pitchfork, a shovel and a wheelbarrow. Your stable should be well ventilated without being drafty, have good drainage and floors that can be kept clean with minimum effort. You should have storage space for hay, grain and bedding (straw or shavings) and accessible water. A horse, depending on size and the season, may drink from five to fifteen gallons of water a day. Even though you have highly-desirable pasture land grass is not enough for a healthy working horse—his diet must include oats, corn, an occasional bran mash, and of course, hay. There should be salt in his stall or pasture. The average horse, getting regular exercise, may eat between fifteen and twenty pounds of hay a day and from six to twelve pounds of oats. Unfortunately, you can't just toss in his ration and forget him; a horse, for his size, has a small stomach, and should be fed often. His food should be divided into three meals a day (some stables feed smaller amounts five times a day).

A Clean Stall

The stall should be cleaned once a day, and picked out

more often if possible. Thrush, a decay of the foot, is caused when the horse is left standing in damp, dirty bedding. The horse's hoofs, of course, should be cleaned daily when he has his daily grooming. Most horses will allow you to handle their feet as long as you don't hurt them. Always start cleaning the foot around the edges—following the line of the shoe and hoof wall. The center, frog section of the foot is more tender, and around that area work from the heel toward the point of the frog—gently.

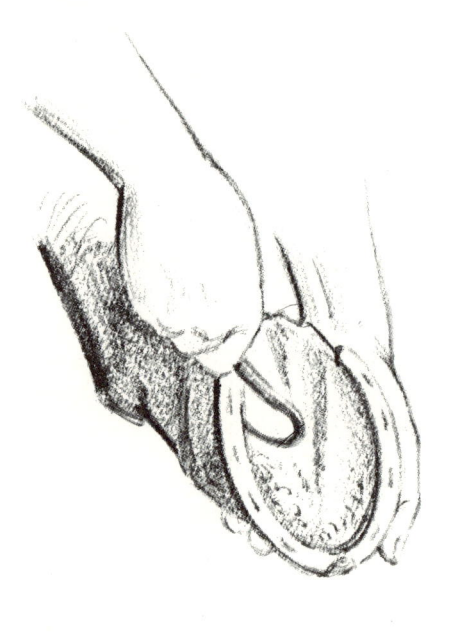

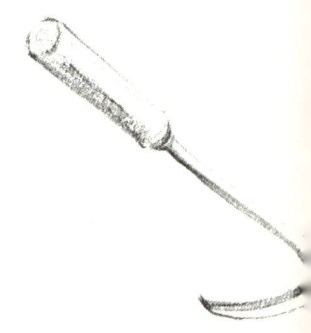

GROOMING YOUR HORSE

Even though you don't ride the horse every day, his coat should have some care—a once-a-week brushing leaves a dull, dandruff-infested coat. Daily grooming, even for five or ten minutes, will develop a coat with the luster of highly polished furniture. Your stable area should have some sort of cross-tie arrangement—ropes with snaps to hook on the rings on each side of his halter. With a horse cross tied, you can work around him in safety. In cleaning, stand at his side and work from head to tail.

You can develop ambidextrousness by starting with the comb, brush or rag in the left hand for the head, neck and shoulder area (when you are on his left side) and switching your equipment to the right hand as you work back to the hindquarters. By standing still and using both hands, you will not get flicked in the face by his tail when he is chasing flies or stepped on or kicked when he is using his hoofs for the same purpose. Get into the habit of crossing *in front* of the horse when you want to work on the other side.

Seasonal Problems

Winter-time grooming is more of a problem as the coat is heavier and longer. Keeping a horse well-blanketed will cut down some on the wooly growth, but come spring you will find your horse shedding and you having more work . . . but not much more if you have combed and brushed him regularly. In warm weather there is no reason why you should not give your horse a bath. Use ordinary shampoo and buckets of warm water. Rub him dry with rags, walk him a bit, and be sure he is not in a draft when he is put away. His tail and mane should be washed whenever they appear to need it, unless it is freezing cold. Incidentally, a horse's coat will sunburn; provide cover on hot days.

Saddling Your Horse

Once your horse is cleaned up, you are ready to ride. Put on the saddle first. As with all actions around horses, approach him from the left side. Be certain that the girth is pulled over the top of the saddle and held on your side, lest it fly and hit the horse. Standing by the shoulder, facing the hindquarters, hold the pommel area in the left hand and the cantle in the right. A flick of the wrist and the saddle is on. Once the saddle is set, it is worth the few extra steps to walk around the other side to be sure that the girth is flat and that none of the billet straps has twisted. Then back on the left side, reach under and pick up the girth and buckle it loosely and evenly. Then draw it up gradually until you think it is as snug as it should be. Unbuckle the halter, slip it off the horse's head and rebuckle it around his neck. That way he is attached at all times until you have him bridled and are ready to mount.

Securing the Bridle

Take the headpiece of the bridle in the right hand and line up the bits in the left. Most horses will open their mouths and take the bits without any trouble, but be sure that the bits are in the mouth *before* slipping the headpiece over the ears. If something delays you before mounting, do *not* snap the cross ties to the bridle. Put the halter on over the bridle and snap the ties in the accustomed rings.

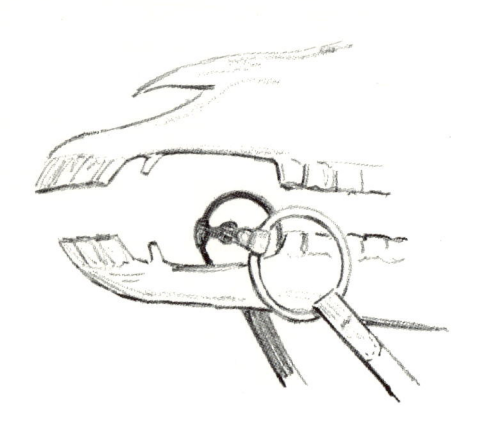

After the Ride

After the ride, simply reverse the process. The bridle comes off first. If you have a bucket of water handy, dip the bit at once; this rinsing may save you some work later. Then take off the saddle, and depending on how much the horse is sweating, either go over him with a scraper (same position as for cleaning) or rub him down with a rag. You can sponge the saddle area, the bridle area, the nostrils and mouth with warm water. Then, if he is still hot, put a cooler or a sheet on him and walk the horse slowly until he has dried out completely and is breathing normally. Do *not* give him feed or water until that time. And when you lead him into his stall, be sure and walk all the way in with him, turn him around so that his head is toward the door, and then unsnap the lead. In that way you can never be kicked—accidentally or on purpose.

After the horse has been cared for, give a few minutes to your tack. Again, it will save you time in the long run. Sponge off the inside of the saddle—dirty, stiff saddles cause sores on the horse's back, while well-soaped saddles and bridles remain soft and flexible for years and withstand occasional rain soakings. Now you can sit down and relax. And if you really like your horse, all this won't seem a bit like work, but rather a rewarding pleasure.

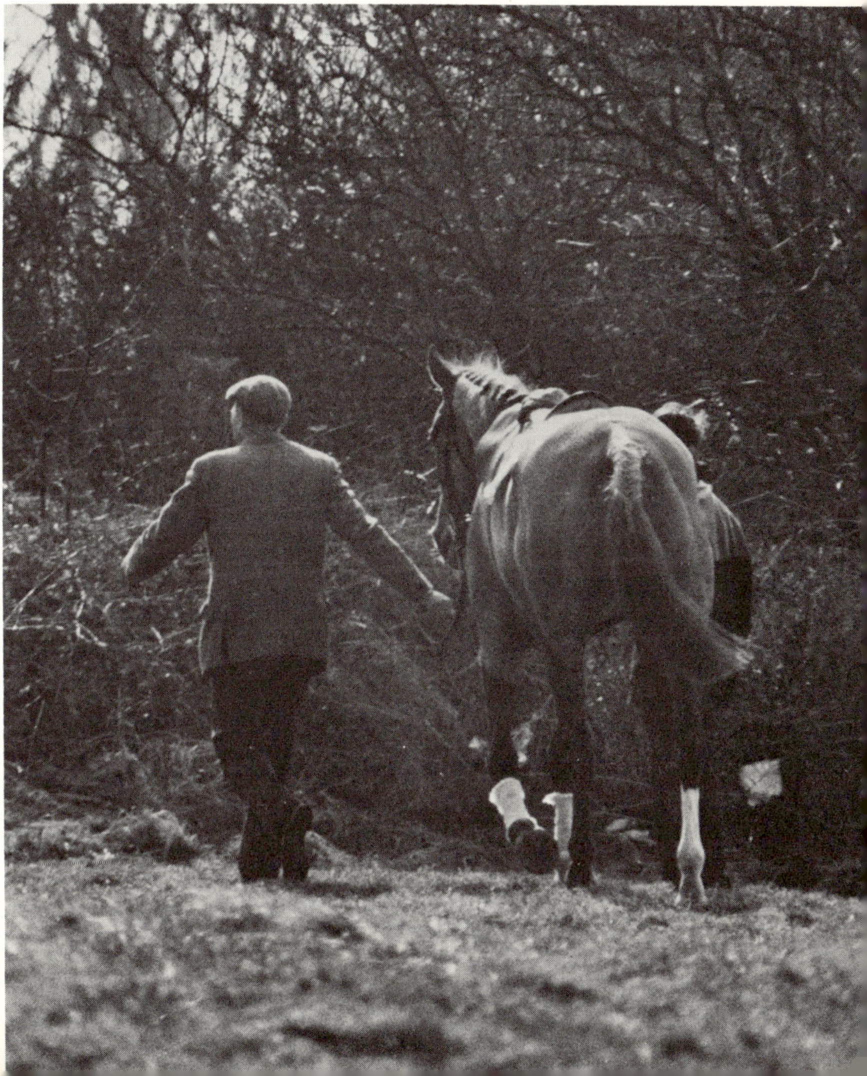